Rule breaker.

Chance taker.

Troublemaker.

AMAZING GRACE.

To my daughters, Kim and Lisa. —L.W.

For my mother, who has always supported me, and for the women
who strive to make the future a better place for young girls everywhere. —K.W.

STERLING CHILDREN'S BOOKS
New York

An Imprint of Sterling Publishing Co., Inc.
1166 Avenue of the Americas
New York, NY 10036

STERLING CHILDREN'S BOOKS and the distinctive Sterling Children's Books logo
are registered trademarks of Sterling Publishing Co., Inc.

Text © 2017 by Laurie Wallmark
Illustrations © 2017 by Katy Wu

ISBN 978-1-4549-2000-7

Library of Congress Cataloging-in-Publication Data

Names: Wallmark, Laurie. | Wu, Katy, illustrator.
Title: Grace Hopper : queen of computer code / by Laurie Wallmark ;
    illustrated by Katy Wu.
Description: New York : Sterling Children's Books, [2017] | Audience: Age 8.
    | Includes bibliographical references.
Identifiers: LCCN 2016035342 | ISBN 9781454920007
Subjects: LCSH: Hopper, Grace Murray--Juvenile literature. | Women
    admirals--United States--Biography--Juvenile literature. |
    Admirals--United States--Biography--Juvenile literature. | Women computer
    engineers--United States--Biography--Juvenile literature. | Computer
    engineers--United States--Biography--Juvenile literature.
Classification: LCC V63.H66 W35 2017 | DDC 359.0092 [B] --dc23 LC record available at https://
lccn.loc.gov/2016035342

Distributed in Canada by Sterling Publishing Co., Inc.
c/o Canadian Manda Group, 664 Annette Street
Toronto, Ontario, Canada M6S 2C8
Distributed in the United Kingdom by GMC Distribution Services
Castle Place, 166 High Street, Lewes, East Sussex, England BN7 1XU
Distributed in Australia by NewSouth Books
45 Beach Street, Coogee, NSW 2034, Australia

For information about custom editions, special sales, and premium and corporate purchases, please contact
Sterling Special Sales at 800-805-5489 or specialsales@sterlingpublishing.com.

Manufactured in China

Lot #:
2 4 6 8 10 9 7 5 3 1
03/17

www.sterlingpublishing.com

The artwork for this book was created digitally.
Design by Irene Vandervoort

GRACE HOPPER
Queen of Computer Code

Written by **Laurie Wallmark**   Illustrated by **Katy Wu**

STERLING CHILDREN'S BOOKS
New York

Grace leaned back in her chair and yawned.
Once again she had worked far into the night
writing computer code.

Grace's latest computer program, one to guide
Navy missiles, was almost complete. All that
was left was to check her work. Grace
reviewed the code line
by line, making sure she
hadn't made any mistakes.

When she finished, Grace set down her pencil and frowned. The last section of her program, a bit of code that multiplied numbers, looked familiar. She checked back through her work and found she had written that same code before. Over and over and over again.

Grace snorted. What a colossal waste of time! There had to be a better way. Why not make the computer do the work? Computers were good at doing boring jobs.

"[I was] lazy as all get out. I never wanted to do anything over again."

She figured out a way to store pieces of a program, like her multiplication code, inside the machine. When she needed to use that code in another program, all Grace had to do was tell the computer where to find it. The computer then joined together the many bits of code into one complete program.

No one had ever done that before. Grace was the first.

Even as a child, Grace loved to tinker with gadgets and learn new ideas. She wanted to understand how things worked so she could make them better.

When Grace was seven she unscrewed the back of her alarm clock and took a peek. She reached in and . . .

Out popped a spring, followed by several gears. One rolled across the floor and under her bed.

Grace scooped up the parts and tried to put them back together. No matter which piece she put where, she couldn't get the clock to run.

She needed another
clock she could study,
one that still worked.

Grace sprinted from room to room.
Clock by clock, she fiddled with gears
and springs, levers and pins. She arranged
them this way and that.

Seven clocks later, seven-year-old Grace
understood what made clocks tick.

When Grace's mother discovered the many jumbles of clock parts scattered around the house, all she could do was laugh. After all, Grace was just being Grace.

Once Grace figured out how clocks worked, she moved on to bigger challenges. She followed a complicated blueprint and constructed a dollhouse made of stone. But there were no stairs. How could her dolls get to the top floor?

"If you've got a good idea, and you know it's going to work, go ahead and do it."

Not a problem for junior-engineer Grace. She opened her toy construction kit and laid out everything she'd need—nuts, bolts, metal pieces, and an electric motor. It took some experimentation, but Grace figured it out. Now her dolls had an elevator to go upstairs.

Grace delighted in learning difficult concepts—the harder the better. While her schoolmates wore frilly dresses and learned to be young ladies, Grace studied math and science. Her bedroom overflowed with books and scientific equipment.

She raced through her high school classes and finished two years early. Grace couldn't wait to start college.

More classes. More learning. More fun!

On the day her college entrance grades arrived, Grace's hands trembled. She ripped open the envelope and proudly read aloud to her parents the many high marks in math and science.

When she reached the grade for Latin, Grace fell silent.

Failed! She had failed Latin!

Without Latin, Grace couldn't go to college. Without college, Grace couldn't be a mathematician. Without math, Grace couldn't be Grace.

Grace waved to her schoolmates as they left for college without her. Nothing would stop her from joining them next year. She held her head high and returned to her studies. Working hard, Grace even conquered Latin. At the end of the year she passed all her exams.

With her trunks packed and her math books in hand, Grace left for Vassar College, an all-women's school. Some of her classmates took classes called "Husbands and Wives" and "Motherhood," but not Grace. Her favorite subjects were math and physics.

Grace did more in college than just study. Whenever there was fun or adventure to be found, she was always first in line. Her personal motto was: "Dare and Do." When a barnstormer came to town offering plane rides, Grace rushed to sign up.

"I squandered all my money—... it cost $10— and went up in the plane."

She pulled herself up into the seat behind the pilot and adjusted her goggles. With a deafening roar the propeller sputtered into action. The biplane rattled across the field and lifted off. With each loop-the-loop through the air, Grace's grin grew wider and wider.

Because of Grace's hard work and intelligence, the other students respected her abilities. They often came to her for help with their studies.

One day her fellow students entered the room, only to see a bathtub filled to the brim with water. Grace invited a volunteer to step into the tub, clothes and all. Water sloshed over the edges and flooded the floor.

The students burst into laughter.

Grace explained the reason for this tidal wave;
the volume of the student's body pushed out the
same volume of water.

The result? One soggy student, wrapped in a towel,
and one math lesson, never forgotten.

When Grace moved on to graduate school at Yale University, there was only one other woman in her class. This didn't bother Grace in the least.

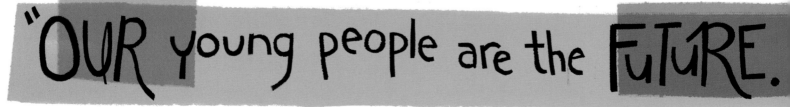
"OUR young people are the FUTURE.

Grace wanted to share her passion for math, so she took a job teaching at Vassar College. Her classes were always both practical and fun.

Even though Grace loved teaching, America was now at war and needed the best mathematicians to design weapons. Patriotic Grace wanted to help her country, so she tried to enlist in the Navy.

That proved to be a problem.

We must PROVIDE for them."

Based on the Navy's requirements for new recruits at the time, Grace was too old and too skinny to enlist. She was 36 and weighed only 105 pounds. Grace could be very persuasive, however. It took her more than a year, but Grace convinced the Navy that they needed her.

"FAITHFULNESS IN ALL THINGS

MY MOTTO IS YOU SEE:

"The world will be a better place
When all agree with me."

Because of her superior math skills Grace was assigned to write programs for one of the first computers ever built, the Mark I. Only a few people had ever programmed before, so she had to learn how to do it on her own.

One late summer day a coworker burst into Grace's office. The new computer, the Mark II, had stopped working.

She gasped! This had never happened before. Not with any of *her* programs.

Grace thought it had to be a prank. After all, she loved playing jokes on her coworkers. Maybe the other engineers were getting their revenge.

But they weren't. The computer really wasn't working.

For hours Grace and her team reviewed the code, but could find no error. It was as if the green ceramic gremlin that always sat in Grace's office had come to life and sneaked into the machine to make mischief.

That was it!

Maybe the problem wasn't in her program. Maybe it was in the computer.

Grace jumped to her feet and hurried down the hall. The immense computer room usually thrummed with the click of metal switches and whir of paper tape. Today all was silent.

"I HAVE INSATIABLE CURIOSITY.
It's solving problems.
Every time you solve a
problem, another one
shows up behind it.
That's the challenge."

Grace and her team searched everywhere for the problem. Grace used her pocket mirror to check inside the machine. She angled it this way and that. No matter where the engineers looked, they didn't see anything wrong. No loose wires or stray sparks. Not even a naughty gremlin.

The engineers were stumped. They had checked everything. What could be causing the problem?

Then someone saw it—a moth was trapped inside, blocking a switch from working properly.

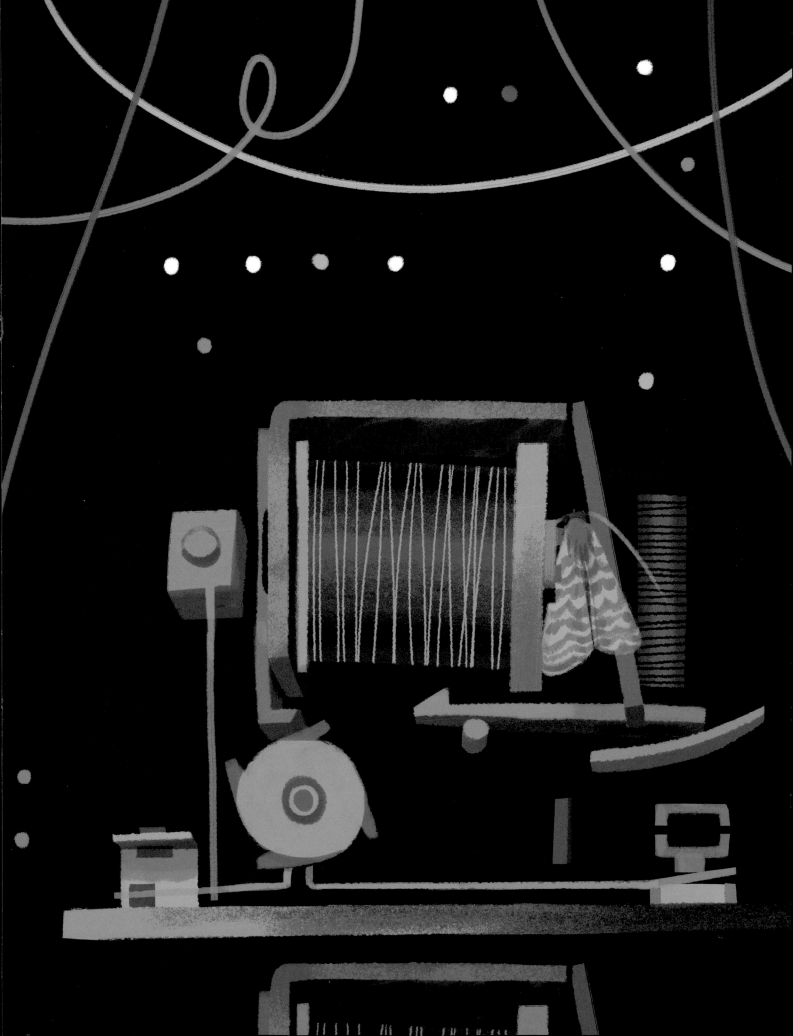

One of the engineers borrowed Grace's eyebrow tweezers and removed the dead moth. The computer started up again with no problem.

Being good scientists, Grace and her team taped the moth into the logbook to record their unusual finding. They added a note, "First actual case of [a computer] bug being found."

Ever since then, because of Grace's sense of humor, computer glitches have been called "bugs."

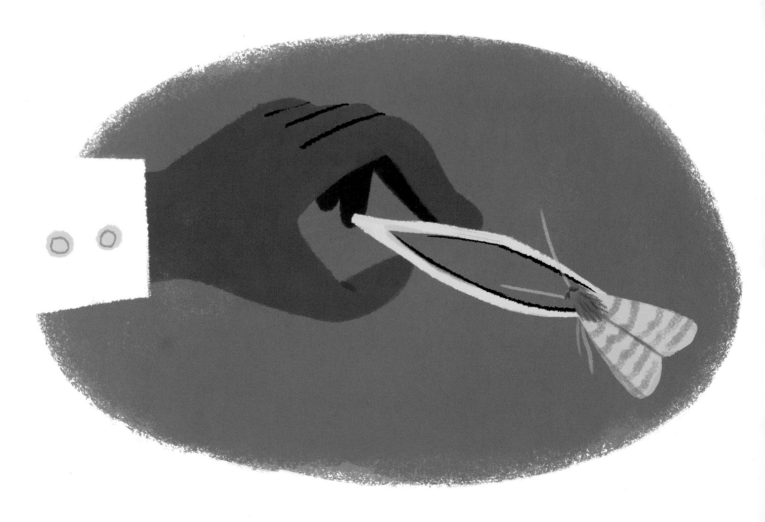

Early computers didn't understand letters or words, only programs filled with lines and lines of "1"s and "0"s. As Grace worked on a brand-new computer called the UNIVAC I, she thought about ways to make programming even easier. Not everyone was as comfortable thinking in numbers as she. Grace wanted anyone to be able to use computers, not just scientists and engineers.

Grace glanced at the wall clock she had rigged to run backward. It reminded her to use her imagination. Unconventional thinking was often the key to solving problems.

Humans are allergic to change. They like to say, "We've always done it this way." I try to fight that.

To allow her brain a chance to consider new ideas, Grace took a break from programming. She doodled cartoons of gremlins and dragons and other fantastical creatures.

While she drew she asked herself questions. Why should people have to learn computer language? Why couldn't computers learn people language?

They could!

Grace invented a program that let people use words to tell the computer what to do. Her program, named FLOW-MATIC, included simple English commands like MULTIPLY. FLOW-MATIC translated MULTIPLY and the other commands into instructions the computer could understand.

This was much easier than programming pages of "1"s and "0"s.
With the help of Grace's program, she and her coworkers were able
to write code more quickly and with fewer errors.

When Grace was sixty years old the Navy forced her to retire. They said she was too old to serve.

"It was the saddest day of my life."

Within a few months they realized their mistake and asked her to return for a short, six-month assignment. This short assignment lasted for twenty years.

Grace, now an admiral, finally retired from the Navy.

For the second time.

At age eighty.

For almost fifty years, Grace Hopper, the Queen of Computer Code, dedicated her life to solving computer problems.

GRACE'S TIMELINE

DECEMBER 9, 1906   Grace Murray is born in New York City.

1914–1918   World War I.

1917   The United States enters World War I.

1928   Graduates with an honors BA degree in mathematics and physics from Vassar College. Inducted into the Phi Beta Kappa honor society.

1929–1939   The Great Depression. (During this period of great financial problems, millions of people were out of work, and many went hungry.)

1930   Graduates with an MA degree in mathematics from Yale University. Marries Vincent Foster Hopper.

1934   Graduates with a PhD in mathematics from Yale University. Inducted into the Sigma Xi scientific honor society.

1931–1943   Teaches mathematics at Vassar College.

1938   Zuse I computer is built in Germany (first functional, general-purpose digital computer).

1939–1945   World War II.

DECEMBER 1941   The United States enters World War II after Japan bombs the Pearl Harbor navy base in Hawaii.

DECEMBER 1943   Is sworn into the WAVES (Women Accepted for Volunteer Emergency Service), the women's branch of the US Navy.

1944   Mark I computer is built (first functional, large-scale, general-purpose computer in America).

1944–1949   Works at the Bureau of Ships Computation Project, Harvard University.

1947   Mark II computer is built.

1949–1971   Works at the Eckert-Mauchly Computer Corporation (later Sperry Rand).

1951 UNIVAC I computer is built.

1953 First thinks of using English words in programs.

1957–1959 Develops FLOW-MATIC for the UNIVAC I computer.

1959 Helps to develop specifications for COBOL (COmmon Business-Oriented Language) based on FLOW-MATIC.

1966 Is forced to retire from the Navy because of her age.

1967 Is recalled to active duty by the Navy.

1967–1977 Works as Director of the Navy Programming Languages Group.

1969 First message is sent over ARPANET (precursor to the Internet).

1975 Altair 8800, considered to be the first personal computer, is introduced to consumers.

1977–1986 Works as Special Staff to NAVDAC, the Naval Data Automation Command.

1983 Is promoted to Rear Admiral, Lower Half (previously called Commodore).

1986 Retires a second time from the Navy, at age 79.

1986–1991 Works at Digital Equipment Corporation.

1991 World Wide Web is introduced to the public.

JANUARY 1, 1992 Grace Murray Hopper dies and is buried at Arlington National Cemetery with full military honors.

OCTOBER 21, 2016 The United States Naval Academy breaks ground on a new building for Cyber Security Studies, which will be named after Grace Hopper when completed in 2019.

NOVEMBER 22, 2016 Awarded the Presidential Medal of Freedom, the nation's highest civilian honor.

SELECTED BIBLIOGRAPHY

Beyer, Kurt W. *Grace Hopper and the Invention of the Information Age.*
Cambridge, MA: MIT Press, 2009.

Billings, Charlene W. *Grace Hopper: Navy Admiral and Computer Pioneer.*
Hillsdale, NJ: Enslow Publishers, 1989.

Schneider, Carl and Dorothy Schneider. *Grace Hopper: Working to Create the Future.*
New York: Sofwest Press, 1998.

Whitelaw, Nancy. *Grace Hopper: Programming Pioneer.*
New York: WH Freeman and Co, 1995.

Williams, Kathleen Boone. *Grace Hopper: Admiral of the Cyber Sea.*
Annapolis, MD: Naval Institute Press, 2004.

ADDITIONAL READING ABOUT OTHER WOMEN IN STEM
(SCIENCE, TECHNOLOGY, ENGINEERING, MATH)

Burleigh, Robert. Illustrated by Raúl Colón. *Look Up! Henrietta Leavitt, Pioneering Woman Astronomer.* New York: Simon & Schuster Books for Young Readers, 2013.

Chin-Lee, Cynthia. Illustrated by Megan Halsey and Sean Addy. *Amelia to Zora: Twenty-Six Women Who Changed the World.* Watertown: Charlesbridge, 2005.

Hopkins, H. Joseph. Illustrated by Jill McElmurry. *The Tree Lady: The True Story of How One Tree-Loving Woman Changed a City Forever.* New York: Beach Lane Books, 2013.

McDonnell, Patrick. *Me . . . Jane.* New York: Little, Brown Books for Young Readers, 2011.

Nivola, Claire A. *Life in the Ocean: The Story of Oceanographer Sylvia Earle.*
New York: Frances Foster Books, 2012.

Stone, Tanya Lee. *Almost Astronauts: 13 Women Who Dared to Dream.*
Somerville: Candlewick, 2009.

Thimmesh, Catherine. Illustrated by Melissa Sweet. *Girls Think of Everything: Stories of Ingenious Inventions by Women.* Boston: HMH Books for Young Readers, 2002.

Wallmark, Laurie. Illustrated by April Chu. *Ada Byron Lovelace and the Thinking Machine.*
San Francisco: Creston Books, 2015.